LANTERN LIT SERIES
VOL. 2

DOG ON A CHAIN PRESS

MICHAEL HAEFLINGER

FRANK REARDON

MIKE MERAZ

Copyright© 2014 Dog On A Chain Press

All rights reserved. This book or any portion thereof may not be reproduced or used in any manner whatsoever without the express written permission of the publisher/author(s) except for the use of brief quotations in a book review.

Printed in the United States of America

First printing 2014

ISBN 978-0-9855291-5-4

Dog On A Chain Press
c/o Beasley Barrenton
503 Silverleaf Rd.
Zionville, NC 28698

For ordering information (Publisher Direct) or all other inquiry
dogonachainpress@yahoo.com
http://dogonachainpress.tumblr.com

for contributor credits/permission see back page(s)

"Let the blood lie, jackal will concur if there be brimstone or ghost."

-Bazzel Bumgarden

The Days Before

Poems by

Michael Haeflinger

The Community Garden

Nothing beats a hard day's work.

Among snap pea trestles
and tomato plant cages,
I breathe deeply
decomposition.

Gone are barges
of iron frame ghost rails,
gone are board-ups
of the imagination.

It's just me
and the dirt
and the morning

and the tall man with the cane
trailing his junky girl
into the sunrise –

I wonder if he knows anyplace to go.

I want to invite him to kneel with me,
to pray to the god of soil:
his cloud angel marionettes,
his bishops of sewer steam.

Across the city, roots burrow infinite
and stems emerge in the misdirection of night.

Across the street, the metal shields
of the liquor store slide into the wall.
Piles of turnip bulbs along the furrow
are only the beginning of a death.

My knees ache and everything
flowers too soon these days.

Margin of Error

A frozen rope is only as good
as the margin of error
in a warbler's song.

Both perch on the fence
as the white-toothed tiger
with a weed-whacker mows his lawn.

Both keep their songs
to themselves.
Both mingle with rot.

Meanwhile, a mulberry blossoms
beneath the footprints,
crickets rise vocal over compost,
pinchers and centipedes
under the log
believe they are scorpions.

What song is the warbler's?

A cloud burst?
A cat prowl?
         A wind chime
caught in a poplar's throat?

Spring Day

how it smells before rain:

turn off the stove
and go to the park
before they lock the gates

when you get home:
chickpeas swimming in cumin,
lukewarm, shedding skins

like heavy coats

Trash Day

Rainfall, a broken piece of floor, linoleum,
recycling to the rim with beer cans,
two neighbor girls off to school,
someplace behind the pull of sky,
a line of buildings dark all day.

Birds leave wings packed,
find treasures spring deposits in the yard:
a basketball hoop crooked as a vulture,
a shopping cart full of dry leaves,
the names of her sons
who'll never see parole
spray painted on the stucco.

Still, she takes her trash out every Monday,
even when the sun refuses her,
her leftovers a precious fortress
on the sloped sidewalk,
the sons of other mothers
rumbling towards her
in great combustible wombs
to take it all away.

Flea Market

At the roadside stand, ten for a dollar.

Insufficient Romances, random bandanas,
      mysteries you've solved
      by page eighty-three.
Campaign buttons
      (everyone lost).
Such determination
      in heroes' eyes.

What breakfast burrito? What Earl Grey
    afternoon?
Patton, king of bergamot, king of every shore,
    peering over the frosted edge of Heaven,
pistol-whipped the photographer
    into falling in love with him.

In this cardboard box on the cardboard table
      not even Patton goes for a dollar.
Not fifty cents for all those
      he slaughtered with a snort.

A dime for the general and a dime for the author,
and one for the redneck booth tender,
    for the dirt beneath his soles.
The old man's dog, the Styrofoam cooler full
    of beer and sandwiches,

for the lawn chair and its heart attack sturdiness,
a dime for the grass dying under the lawn chair,
    how it ruffles the soil's libretto
    into steadfast doubt,
a dime for the open back of his van, a toothless
    mouth of carpet and suggestion,
a dime for the woman in the front seat
    examining her jagged cuticles:
how much longer is this going to take?

Patton's heart could lift a tank off a solider
    with one hand.
No change in his pocket, no trumpets
    blasting taps between his ears, no woman

         to complain about the eager destruction of
                weather.
Still: a dime for Poirot's keychain memory and
         a dime for McKuen's prolificacy.
One for Chandler and One for Krishnamurti,
         to whom money meant nothing and everything
         and still we are not saved.

I fit it all in my backpack, scuffed by the mites
         on the subway floor.
Everything I carry reminds me
         of dead men's chests.
   Ghosts swirl around the barter.

         She fishes another bent cigarette from her
         skin-tight breast pocket.

Commandments

Night is a basket of baby mice,
pink and blind and finite.
And day is a cauldron of witches brew
bubbling over the rim.
All words should come in order,
this is the first commandment.
The second is to love
and the third, to obey.
Countesses and nobodies
line country lanes
to steal the eyes of princes
assumed to seek the counsel
of ancestors.

But the dead see only what we see:
angel ledges and fountain pigeons,
notebooks full of directions,
night that thirsty cat mewing
in the glassy alley.
They float between the space between,
in the quiet moments when the tea
disappears into morning steam,
in the late afternoon when the telephone
loses its will to ring.

Chambered Nautilus

All it is
is breath.
Spun
into its
Fibonacci self,
clinging
to the reef
in the artificial
darkness
of electricity,
it can't help
but pray.
Close up:
a cabbage,
a squid cousin,
a housecat
tapestry
in a shell.
A muscle
and nothing,
a lung
exposing
its essence:
in
out
in out,
while we
pass.

The Dogs Bark Midnight

The dogs bark midnight
        into the hills

And men with heads
        full of glue

climb the hill
        in loose corkscrews

And the morning rooster
        trumpets a chorus

of sunrise cocks
        celebrating day's return

And the sun is some place
        behind that fog

someplace in that fog,
        the sun is

And other birds unseen
        shuffle branches

in their grips, shake their heads,
        wiggle their hips

And the teenagers waking
        in the room next door

giggle when they remember
        the night before:

Fire in the Belly

If I thought it would make a difference,
my head in a circus's worth of lions' mouths,
hair braised in antelope's blood.

Work callouses enough to balance
aluminum rods on my fingertips and spin
eight plates, if I thought it meant you'd stay.

Equally troubling: the low, tangential hum
of the firehouse in the distance
when you are trying to read in bed.

If I thought it mattered, a canvas instead,
an attempt to see the contrast
between near and far away.

Messiah

Who closed his eyes
and saw burning Romans.
A bastard. An only child.
A fuck-up talking shit
to his friends
and the unemployed.
The kid who stayed
in the woods all day.
The kid who
couldn't get along.
The loner
who carved a crescent
into the cheek of night,
who wept for no reason
as his friends slept
in the dance
of a dwindling campfire.

Summer Wind

hey summer wind
don't be fooled
it's June now
you can be subtle

no use in being cold
and full of spite

the trees still standing
still love you

me,
I'm a balloon
with the heart of a street cleaner

I'm a tunnel
with walls of pipe organs

so blow baby blow

hey summer wind
don't be fooled
it's June now
and you are still air

Little Orange Got a Bird

Little Orange got a bird,
either pounced her in the yard
or dragged her in from the alley –
I was late to the show,

fiddling with the radio,
looking for a fist busting open
a face in Cairo, the bluffs
over the rising Mississippi

frowning with sorrow.
Rembrandt is there, too,
his Jewish neighbors
lining up to pose

in briny afternoons
for portraits that will emerge
three hundred years later
as evidence of his doubt.

Later, with a shovel
I will carry the ants
and what remains
of the bird back

to the alley while
Little Orange sleeps
in the shade, full
of beauty and flight.

haiku

citywide sunset
pink cloud disappears
behind an old house

                      in the dark building
                      one light alone through glass
                      before five o' clock

scent of roasting nuts
wafts up the morning staircase
I am so lonesome

                      finger in my nose
                      what great discovery there
                      giggle like a child

plant in the window
gets the most light of them all
still dies in winter

                      behind the clouds, sun
                      so I am led to believe
                      behind the sun, black

Saturday neighbors
already in the street know:
nothing forever

                      a life without work
                      is not the same as working
                      until you're dead

                      the poem is false
                      as soon as it's written down:
                      this poem is false

Here Sits the Devil

here sits the devil,
here stands the boy

here writhes the girl
with a fire-proof toy

here cries the mother,
there was the pa

here plays the daughter
a rusted hand saw

here hangs the savior,
here kneels the friend

'here' is the place they
all go in the end

Going Away Party

her smile is a bag of lightning bugs
on a bedside table

tomorrow she goes home
where the chamber of commerce
welcomes visitors at the city gate
with stacks of dead bodies

but tonight her laugh is an open bottle
of tequila

tonight she watches
coals in the grill go
from red to white
to white to red

Erosion

the final act:
that which
birds lose

formation
and plummet
into the audience.

mosquitos
grow legs
on the ends

of their legs,
bells ring
and no one moves.

the final act:
earth mostly water
becomes wholly water

sifting
bits of earth
it can't digest.

floating in its soil,
subtle moments
before a great autumn.

Resurrection

Walking I think dead
trees without leaves
or brown flimsy paper
leaves I think
slush-piled gutters
whole park of
thousand-armed
skeletons frozen
in their dances

I think rose bush
stop to inhale
shriveled bulbs
waxy thorns I think
exhausted of breath
the day measures short
time to turn hips I think
to move along I think
to sidle between branches

overgrown sidewalk
puddles of ice water
rose thorn reaches
catches pulls
scarf loosens
thread says
hey motherfucker
says hey I'm talking
to you says who
you calling dead, son

Variation on the Seventh Verse

Take away the bus station
with its seven or so entrances
(everything in pairs but the
      main door, bigger and more open
            than the other six or four)

It's impossible to say
how whatever-it-all began.

Handshakes, head nods, requests
for excuse, scents, a symmetrical face,
baby crying, old man needing spare change –
so what?

It doesn't matter if the buses never leave.
They all come back anyway.

Structure of Two Act Plays

A single light bulb

A painted window
                        (sun,
                                 blue sky)

A small dark desk
               A hard bed
                     with hard pillows
                             covered in a menagerie
                             of blankets

A chorus of wives
inching along the fence posts

Bars on the windows,
       windows that slide
              into the cold afternoon

She's here, but I'm not

I'm someplace
                frozen,
I'm on the south pole
of my heart:

A single desk chair,
small dark desk chair

Behind a sheer curtain
beyond a cold desk

There Somewhere

everything and not
everything
somewhere
on the table
near cold cuts
a fly buzzes,
somebody tells
the joke wrong:

a woman with glasses
raised on a farm
with delicate wrists
could never dream
of that kind of output

it's late
and not that
anyone cares

this party
is over

Michael Haeflinger is originally from the Midwest. He currently lives in Tacoma, WA. His first book of poetry, <u>Love Poem For The Everyday</u>, was released by *Dog On A Chain Press* in 2011. His work can be found at www.michaelhaeflinger.com.

Acknowledgments:

These poems have appeared or will appear in the following journals. Many thanks to their editors:

"The Community Garden"
    Creative Colloquy
"Spring Day" and "Going Away Party"
    Four Quarters Magazine
"Commandments"
    Hobo Camp Review

This collection is dedicated to Nissa Lee, a great friend with a keen ear and a lovely vision.

The Broken Halo Blues

Poems by

Frank Reardon

JEREMIAH

Somewhere outside
Tomah, Wisconsin,
upon numb ass,
tired and defiled,
the Amish man
who smelled of bologna
and odd starch
leaned in and asked
if I was a farmer.

His beard of no mustache,
his hat of straw,
his shirt of blue tears,
and his crazy eyes
from another man's nightmare
patiently
awaited my response
with a boot tap.

I contemplated
the question
for a moment
as I watched
the big dipper
touch the new earth
from the night window
of a narrowing
greyhound seat.

Fuck.

SKIPPING DOWN THE AVENUE OF BONES WITH A BOUQUET OF DAFFODILS IN EACH HAND

rather than book sales,
money,
exteriors,
or the vapid
& pretentiousness,
just
let me be
one simple word
of encouragement
flowing
from the chambers
of humility's
beating heart.

KEEP TRYING

As I piss on the empty beer cans
outside the backdoor,
I watch the steam
of all that's still possible
rise up from the ashes
like an angry set of fangs
preparing to bite down on all
that has been given.

NOTE TO CHOPIN

Because you are so beautiful before battle,
because of a small incident due to pills,
I haven't cried in months.
When I say small, I discuss months as minutes.
Before battle, before the rockets shoot my cock off
into the air with images of war-torn sky paintings,
I cry. I cry and shake all over whenever you play,
and not because of a physical appearance or even
a mental condition, which has been a coin toss
at best over the years, but because it excites
the balls to outwit the doctors. I never ran home and
popped the white beauties right away, oh no!
I went home and sat back in victory, victory over
those who controlled the senses and cast me out
of mother's womb. Doctors, a circle of circus clowns,
were the first to see me arrive,
and they'll be there to ship me off,
with a final frantic punch to the solar plexus,
a desolate nocturne pulling away from solitude,
without care, without impressions.
Oh, Chopin, what a life! So frightening
and so impossible with each passing minute,
but oh, so beautiful when contemplating the darkness
hidden within a naked hour.

KATELYN'S ROARING ENGINE

When Katelyn switches the gears
of the large forklift
she exposes a left wrist covered up
by a Jesus fish tattoo.
Her laugh is a roaring diesel engine
as she shouts, "fuck you"
in several different languages
while swinging her meaty gut
out from the driver's seat.
Just the other day, next to the running engine
of the forklift, she told me how she met a cool chick to
hang out with and how next Sunday they'll get drunk
together and listen to country music in her apartment.
She said she shares an apartment with another woman
who works with us, but for reasons unknown she
couldn't tell me who it was.
"I need this," she said to me. "I need a cool woman
to hang out with. There's nobody in this fuckin' town!
Why did I leave Tennessee for this place?"
The 10,000 freckles on her face glowed like stars of
speckled shit when she talked about the woman she was
going to meet next Sunday.
She went on about her new friend for what seemed to be
ages. Although I was happy for her, I was also happy for
myself, because the diminished fire in my own belly also
began to glow just a bit brighter. For months, which
seemed like years to me, it had been missing, gone the
way of the fools, gone the way of the lunatics pissing off
the front porches of the doomed.
Then, in her own happy way, Katelyn slugged me in the
arm, swung her meaty gut back into the forklift
and drove away.
Sometimes when the cold and hate is so deeply rooted
in our bones,
a little flaming bag of shit upon the face
is all we need to get by.

LONELY LARRY

Everyday Larry walks into the lumber yard
with his head down due to years of bad posture.
His hair, fake or not, looks like a blond toupee,
and he twiddles his fingers in mad circles
when he speaks. Mona, the cashier,
calls him "Lonely Larry." She says it whenever
he leaves the room. "Lonely Larry, poor-poor,
Lonely Larry." During the day Larry is a lumber
merchandiser and he takes his job very seriously
even if his corduroy pants are pulled up over
his belly button. He has the looks of a giant Weeble
most days, and he's a massive billowing shit-talker
from years of love lost, every day. While fastening the
Velcro straps on his gray sneakers, Larry likes to remind
me of his youth, how in his 20s he was a ladies' man,
a sure-fire chick magnet. He says it was
all due to his over-use of cologne and gold chains.
I find it hard to believe, especially since his work apron
has his name painted on it with large purple letters
bedazzled in silver rhinestones, though he's done
a great job convincing himself of his prowess.
Whenever Kayla, the woman with the perfect ass, the
woman who can speak perfect French, says "hi," Larry's
fake deep voice turns high-pitched and nasally.
He's 60, but whenever that French painting
struts by with her big black boots he turns
into himself: quiet, nervous, perverted, the shy little boy.
At night Larry is a quiz show genius, a Game Show
Network lunatic. Sitting in his father's old leather
recliner, he tries to solve puzzles on The Wheel of
Fortune while sucking root beer from a straw. "Buy a
vowel!" he shouts as he twists off the top of an Oreo
so he can lick the cream filling. "Why won't she buy a
fucking vowel!?" he asks his purple and yellow canary
sitting in its brass cage, but the bird never replies, it just
sits on a perch rapidly moving its head and chirping a
song. Poor-poor Lonely Larry, the game shows are over

and the symphony has gotten so cruel with night songs
that Larry must go under his bed and pull out the old box
with the frayed cardboard cover.
Inside: ancient comic books that he had saved since
he was a child. And with teeth clenched upon bottom lip,
he savors each action packed square, each crime fighter's
heroic action, each word floating inside its cartoon
bubble. The hands are weak, the sweat is real, the
foreboding feeling in the dark pulls at lost eyes and
surrounds him with panic.
Soon Larry will climb into bed. "Gotta get up at 4 a.m.
and do it all over again," he'll whisper to himself.
It's the same thing each day and night, the perfect
hell on earth, relived day after day and night after night.
The perfect assassin with the perfect bullet,
inching closer and closer by the second until
it burrows in us all
and plants the great seed of denial.

JERUSALEM

After a 3 week whiskey bender,
50% of which I don't recall,
I attended an A.A. meeting I didn't
need to go to, or maybe I did.
There were sad faces lined up around
a room, and they were reading from a blue
A.A. book. One guy even shouted, "It's a
great day to be sober!" I disagreed.
They read an assortment
of rules. They read the '12 Steps'
out loud. They joined hands
and prayed the 'Serenity Prayer'
together. Then came the scary part;
I was forced to listen to 45 minutes
of individual stories. Some stories
were overly dull, while others were action
packed. One old man named Ernie
talked about quitting cold turkey
and hallucinations. He talked about
his love for codeine and other assorted
drugs. Another guy named Russ
talked about receiving electric shock therapy
when he was younger. A young woman named
Loretta, who had a marvelous ass,
stood up and talked about losing
her license and how she thinks
about drinking every day. "No shit!"
I said to myself as I shook from last
night's hangover. Another woman
named Stephanie said she missed
driving around at night drinking
12 packs. She said she was amazed
that she was never once pulled over,
but she always ended up in the bed
of some strange man she'd never seen
before. I said to myself, "Where were you when
I was 18?" Then they looked at me

to share a story. I told them I didn't
have one and I was just checking
the place out. They told me not
to be scared. I sighed the sigh
of the defeated and told them I was
currently hungover and that all the Jesus
stuff was sort of freaking me out.
"We don't believe in any one god,"
they replied. I asked, "Then what's with
all the 'Lord's Prayer' stuff?"
"It's just something we like to do,
something that helps us get by,"
they responded. I had nothing else to say
or to reply with. The session was over,
and they all stood around the room.
They began congratulating one another
on making it through another day
sober. Myself, I stood in the corner
waiting for it to all end. Coming here
was a bad idea, I thought to myself.
The worst idea I had since I tried
to jump my BMX bike over my dad's
car engine. It might be even worse
I thought, at least when I jumped
my dad's car I only broke my arm.
This place was sucking out my soul,
decapitating it, and mounting it on
the wall like a prized kill from an African
safari. The party was starting to break
up when the same guy yelled once more,
"It's a great day to be sober!" "Blah!"
I shouted to myself. When the 1st person
finally began to leave, I decided it was a good
time for me to shuffle out, and just
as I was ready to open the door, ready
to feel the sweet freedom of sunshine,
the electric shock therapy guy
came up to me. "We hope to see
you back at the next meeting!"

I didn't respond. I just slightly
shook my head in some derelict
fashion. "Here's a new comer's packet,"
he said, while handing me a massive
envelope stuffed with fliers and schedules.
I took the packet, shook his hand,
and left. When I finally reached the warm
streets, I looked at the packet
and noticed his phone number on
the outside of the envelope. It
said, "Call if you ever need to, anytime
of the day." It only lasted an hour, but
it felt like I just did 10 days in a lock up
facility. I had the shakes something awful,
whiskey benders will do that to a man,
so I walked right down the street
to The Miracle Mart Liquor Store
and bought two nips of fine Canadian
Black Velvet whiskey, and as I unscrewed
the first one I tossed the packet
into the garbage and started to drink
it. Almost immediately I felt the sweet
harsh rolling down my throat
and the burn entering my lungs.
Within moments I felt human again,
less anxious, less hostile, less angry
at god. I guess the liquor store
wasn't called The Miracle Mart
for nothing. I didn't see any miracles
inside the A.A. meeting, just people
who wished they could still drink,
just people stuffing their own pleasures
into envelopes, empty pockets,
and purses full of tissues. I asked
myself, "Where's the miracle in any of that?"
I shook my head in disgust, threw the 1st empty nip on
the ground, opened the 2nd one,
and slowly sipped from it
while I walked the long mile back home to Jerusalem.

BEAUTIFUL NOOSE

There are beautiful nooses,
there are heartbreaking
Patsy Cline songs,
there are empty beer cans,
there are whiskey bottles,
and there is always an endless supply
of pain pills,
but the better solutions,
the A.A. solutions,
or the N.A. solutions,
won't remove the heartache
and they won't remove
the constant stomach pain.
So, I'll keep on reading
William Saroyan,
Kerouac, or the next
small press hero
in order to keep my mind
in shape.
I'll keep pretending
and trying to remember
that life is too precious
when in reality
life is worse than any battlefield
that Louis Celine
could ever imagine.
Life, emotion, sanity;
it's all bullshit.
Struggle is bullshit,
humanity is bullshit,
but instead of hanging
myself, instead of giving
you all the glory, I'll just
piss into the garbage can
and spell your name out
upon the empty
turkey burger box,

I'll surround it
with a crooked heart
and shout fuck you
with the most gorgeous
exclamation point
ever created!

QUARRY STONES

Exhausted, I sit down on quarry stones.
I shiver out a grip of musical dirt
I do not want to search for any reason within,
which is bubbling up inside of the frail books I hold.
I take photographs, bad ones, the grasshoppers
are bashful, so is the praying mantis standing
next to me. He's ready to devour me if need be,
his small stick frame casts a shadow over mica stone.
He's burdened, just as I, he tilts his head, I breathe.
The two of us: dark nurses ready to heal.

BLUEGRASS BABY

She likes to dance on the back deck
in her tight jeans and listen
to Bluegrass: Bill Monroe, Earl Scruggs,
Lester Flatt. She spins in circles.
Her hair, an array of sharp knives,
cuts through the sun and splatters
it all over the sky. She's fast banjo honey.
She's still spinning.

AWOKEN

break the spine
     love the woman
          turning   words

inside
    out.

MONTE SANO MOUNTAIN

Where Steffany and I agreed
to get married.

Where we fucked on the empty
trails in piles of leaves against
a tree or next to one of the streams.

Where I signed our divorce
papers on Mother's Day.

Where the yoga instructor
threw up on my lap
in the front seat of her new Volvo
after I came in her mouth
from another one of her terrible blow jobs.

Where I camped/lived in a tent
and read shitty books
into the night, surviving only
off of oranges, apples,
and bathroom water.

Where I wondered about the cruel
meaning of life
as I watched many sunrises.

Where I picked myself up
and sighed long smoke screens
during many sunsets.

Where I got so drunk during
my daughter's 3rd birthday party
that I was carried off to someone's car
and told to sleep it off
as everyone else sang 'happy birthday.'

Where I went to try

and understand
the death of my sister
with folded hands and many
cigarettes.

Where I cursed God,
where I blamed everyone else
but myself,
where I accepted my own
misfortunes and bad luck.

Where I tried to escape who
I was, where I tried to create
new personas, where I tried
to be anyone other than myself.

Where I stopped abusing
pills and whiskey
and just walked for hours
upon hours and learned
to smile, even if just a tiny
crooked one.

Where I learned to punch
intense winds and cry like a baby
in thickets of trees.

Where I learned about hope
from an old man
who told me that leaning forward
too much will only
keep the eyes clouded
with dust.

Where I was able to open
up my chest with my hands
and feel the bloody pulp like
beat of my own heart.

Where I whittled my first
hiking stick
with deep breaths
and a pocket knife.

Where I tried out my very 1st
pair of hiking boots
that I bought with my first
pill-sober job.

Where I sat on benches
and watched children
play for hours
on the jungle gym.

Where I was finally
reminded
that I too was once
someone's father.

Where I found the old
ax handle,
picked it up and bashed it
over and over
against a tree
until I collapsed
muscle tired and weeping.

Where I realized,
with a mind full of horrors,
that Lilly is the only cure
to my madness.

Where I started
to photograph
colorful flowers
with shaky hands
for the fun of it.

Where I wrote god awful
poetry
and laughed at it
and myself
for long periods
of time.

Where I watched brave Jack,
with pack and tiny tent,
leave Dayton's back patio
and enter the woods
with a careless whistle.

Where I sat with Steffany
8 years later,
crying, hugging
and confessing all our
wrong doings
for hours.

Myself 40, her 36,
a lot of time had passed,
less hair, more wrinkles,
but it was as if she was
still 22 and I was 26.

The same stream
that once rushed
by our feet in 2001
was still rushing by our feet
in 2014.

Life goes on just as is,
moving forward, through pain,
love, hate, agony, death,
rebirth and freedom.

Monte Sano Mountain:
where they will one day spread my ashes.

Frank Reardon: born in 1974 in Boston, Massachusetts and spent his first 28 years living there. Since then, he has lived all over the country, in places such as Alabama, Kansas City and Rhode Island. He is currently living in the Badlands of North Dakota. Frank has been published in various reviews, journals and online zines. His first poetry collection titled: *Interstate Chokehold*, was published by *NeoPoiesis Press* in 2009. The second titled: *Nirvana Haymaker* was published by *NeoPoiesis Press* in 2012. His third collection of poetry was released in November of 2013 titled: *Blood Music* from *Punk Hostage Press*.

Rummage Sale Heart Shapes

Poems by

Mike Meraz

Stride

there is this woman
talking to me
(currently)
she has nice
legs
she whispers
with her eyes
she is married
and lonely
her husband
tells her on the
phone
"my girlfriend
is here, I'll
talk to ya later."
she takes it
in stride
she takes
everything
in
stride.

A New Creature

a new creature
is just an old creature
in a different guise,
wearing a different skin,
talking in a different voice
speaking the same words
just in different colors
and textures.

hand out stretched,
saying hello,
intimating platitudes
is the same person
that infiltrated your being
two years ago,

this time only
younger,

brighter,

more willing
to do damage.

**Cheap Ass Poem On A Friday Night
Because I Was Bored**

this is my
"now I'm really pissed off" hair cut
and these are my
"never been in your room" shoes
and this is my
"everywhere but in the national publications" pen
and these are my
"never will be immortal" thoughts
being read by your
"how does he get away with this shit" eyes.

Note To A Friend Who Had Once Made My Heart Smile:

you
have
lost
your
edge.

Eve

Eve
is
off
somewhere
with
Lucifer.

Adam
is
wondering,

"where is she?"

A Love Poem:

one
cares.

one
does
not.

I
love
her.

she
loves
him.

some
other
girl,

I care
nothing
about,

loves
me.

Distance Bridged By Poetry

I am here.
you are not here.
you are reading my poem.

How

a guy at work asked me how I picked up women.

I told him, "I tell them I'm a writer."

"really?" he asked surprised.

"yeah," I told him, "I play the tortured soul, the guy who writes poetry. some girls really fall for it."

"wow," he said, "I would have never thought of that. do you read them poetry too?"

"no," I said, "I never read girls poetry."

"well," he said, "you do not seem like the type of guy who is good with women but you do have a way."

"yeah," I said, "it's great, but there is one bad side to it."

"what's that?" he asked.

"well often times these girls actually fall in love with me."

"nuh uh"

"yeah, they get all weird and pathetic and want to take walks on the beach, sit on my lap and sing me love songs."

"really?"

"yeah, really, so now when I am out trying to pick up women I just tell them I'm in sales. this way they know I'm only in it for a good time."

Madame Butterfly

Madame Butterfly
(the humming chorus),
and peace
and God
and learned lessons.
a young girls heart aches
in San Pedro,
and in other places.

if they only knew,
they would not cry,
at least,
not so much.

You Are Beautiful, Don't Let Anyone Tell You Different

your eyes write books
your mouth plays songs
your body is an orchestra

you are not one
that needs to create
you are a creation

be still
and wondrous.

Only A Writer

a girl, Italian, big hips,
tattooed legs, comes in
my store every week
to buy groceries.

I've been meaning to talk
to her but all I get out is:

"can I help you?"

and

"uh, excuse me..."

and all I can get out of her
is:

"no..."

and

"mhmm..."

though our conversations are short,
I feel we have something going on,
a little pitter patter floods my heart
every time I see her.

I must think of something
suave to say to her,
something clever,

like in one of my poems
where a light shines
at the end
and a smile enters
the heart.

The Curse Of The Ages

get ready for heartbreak
cause here she comes
bending down
ordering a sandwich
leaning over a shopping cart
glancing to the left
glancing to the right
all those wonderful things she does
(how can a girl be that pretty?)
I stand, pretending not to care
I have seen her before
and her smile made my last four years
but now it's just plain cruel
for that is all she gives me
or will ever give me
I wave hoping to get her attention
"how are you?" I say
"good" she replies
as she glances away
(polite disinterest)
I walk away
hating she is not mine
but some other guys
who is probably as comfortable around her
as he is with his own mother

as for me
my heart is caught in my throat
all the blood in my body
is holding a five minute meeting in my face
there is nothing I can do about it.

the curse of the ages:
wanting something so much
it makes you unable to have it.

Bookstore

I went out looking for
D.H. Lawrence.

I came home with
Villon and Carl Sandburg.

reminds me of a date
I once had
about 3 years ago.

I'm A Genius, You Know

she started to tell me
what is wrong with my writing.
"you're good," she said,
"but you lack detail."
"of course."
"you write like you are talking
rather than in story form."
"yes," I said.
"you're full of bull shit."
"uh huh."
"you need to use more metaphors."
"indeed."

"how come you don't
get your stuff out there?"
I asked her.
"I have submitted to magazines,"
she said.
"well, how about on a blog.
you know blogs are popular these days.
and it give others a chance to check out your work."
"no," she said, "I am too good for a blog.
I want to be published by a real publisher.
I'm a genius you know."
"oh," I said.

she is no longer writing.
she lives with an old man in Mexico.
they have two kids and a dog named Chico.
she still hasn't been published.
and no one has yet to read her work.

The Real Poet

I am at a target range,
there is a young kid
of 19, he shoots he misses.
another man of 29
tries to hit the target
and misses as well.

a madman comes up behind us
and kills us all.

Rainbows, Come Back

I need eyes,
I have chased away
all my rainbows,
called "fools"
the ones I love.

I need eyes,
eyes that can see
reality,
rather than this
dull mist,
this bedroom of horrors.

rainbows, come back.

Yes

how long has
it been since
you've
been in love?

she asked me.

3 years, I told her.

that's a long time,
she said.

the gaps get
longer as you
get older.

how does it feel
now?

like a drug
I've been
without

or a dance
I haven't danced
in a long time.

the mambo
the two step
the waltz
the tango.

the let loose of the brain,
the freedom, the glow.

wow, she said,
you needed this.

yes.

Mike Meraz lives and writes in Los Angeles, California. His book of poems *Watching It Burn* was published by *Dog On A Chain Press* in 2012. His most recent book *43* was published by *Epic Rites* in 2014.

ABOVE PHOTO RENDITION: GABRIEL SANTERNO

COVER IMAGE: STENCIL/SPRAY PAINT BY JASON GOULD: JASONGOULDART.COM

COVER INPUT/LAYOUT: ABBY WHITE-GOULD, A MOST ESTEEMED CONFIDANT OF THE PUBLISHER.

THE MANUSCRIPTS FOR THIS -LANTERN LIT SERIES- HAVE BEEN PERSONALLY SOUGHT FOR THEIR PELT, AND SELECTED BY ME WITH GREAT INTEREST AND APPRECIATION FOR POETS THAT I AM GENUINELY ENTHRALLED TO WORK WITH, POETS THAT ARE POETS AT THE BASIS AND GNARL OF THEIR BEING, POETS WHO CANNOT HELP BUT BE SUCH, POETS THAT WILL CONTINUE SINGING THE GOSPEL, THE GOSPEL OF WHICH WE WILL ALWAYS BE SINGING, POETS COMMANDING THE SHIP FROM WHEREVER IT IS THAT THEY MAY DELIBERATE, ROARING OUT TO A BIRD ON THE WIRE AS IF THAT BIRD IS EVERYMAN AT THE PIER OF THEIR OWN EXISTENCE.

KEEP A LANTERN LIT,
Beasley Barrenton

www.ingramcontent.com/pod-product-compliance
Lightning Source LLC
Chambersburg PA
CBHW031422040426
42444CB00005B/675